Welcome

One of the most exhilarating cities in the world, London is steeped in history whilst embracing innovation. Its skyline is a mix of old and new, with the beautiful architectural splendour of St Paul's Cathedral sitting comfortably alongside the staggering modernity of new high rises. Running through its heart is the River Thames, both joining and separating the city. At 215 miles (346 km), it is England's longest river. The pomp and ceremony of quintessential British culture remains very much on show, from Changing the Guard to the Lord Mayor's Show and tea at The Ritz. With world-famous museums, art galleries, theatres, eight royal parks, shops, restaurants and a buzzing nightlife, London has something on offer for everyone.

Westminster

The political heart of London beats in Westminster and its neo-Gothic Houses of Parliament. This wonderful sightseeing area is also home to the beautiful Westminster Abbey, which, amongst other delights, houses the oldest door in the UK.

There's nothing more 'London' than the vista of Big Ben and the **Houses of Parliament** (known correctly as the New Palace of Westminster) especially when they are lit up at night and the fabulous façade glows with light.

The Houses of Parliament are central to political Britain. The House of Commons and the House of Lords propose and discuss new legislation and the pressing current matters of the day. When Parliament is in session, visitors are able to attend debates. A notice board at the entrance indicates the topics to be discussed that day. Even if you do not venture within, time can be spent marvelling at Sir Charles Barry's architecture, including the Victoria Tower, Central Tower and iconic Clock Tower.

An aerial view of the iconic Houses of Parliament and Westminster Abbey overlooking the River Thames

Guided tours are available that include the Commons Chamber, Lords Chamber, Central Lobby, St Stephen's Hall and medieval Westminster Hall. Westminster Hall is the oldest building on the Parliamentary site and has been central to British history for over 900 years.

The Elizabeth Tower is the most famous sight in the Houses of Parliament, also known as **Big Ben**, named after the bell in the tower, which in turn was named after the Tower's commissioner of works, Benjamin Hall. The Big Ben bell weighs 13 tonnes and a light is shone from the top of the 96-metre (314ft) clock tower to signify when Parliament is in session. Ben has been ringing across Westminster since 1859.

LOOK OUT FOR...

The 137-metre-high (450ft) **London Eye**, erected to mark the millennium, soars above Jubilee Gardens. Each rotation is a graceful 30 minutes and offers a fantastic view of London; there is even an option to enjoy a glass of champagne at the top.

Westminster Abbey

Steeped in more than 1000 years of history, Westminster Abbey is an essential must-see of any day trip to London. It has been the setting for every coronation since 1066 and numerous other royal occasions, including the funerals of Diana, Princess of Wales, and the Queen Mother and sixteen royal weddings.

Left: The intricate gothic façade of Westminster Abbey
Below: Westminster Abbey's interior is just as stunning as its exterior, boasting the highest nave in England

Westminster Abbey (or the Collegiate Church of St Peter, Westminster, to give it its correct title) is an architectural gothic masterpiece of the 13th–16th centuries and a unique witness of British history that has been a place of worship since AD 960. It comprises the shrine of St Edward the Confessor, the tombs of kings and queens and countless memorials to the famous.

Originally a monastery for Benedictine monks, the abbey and many of the building's features attest to this collegial past. The abbey was re-founded by Edward the Confessor, but most of what is visible today was built under the auspices of Henry III, between 1220 and 1272. The exterior of the abbey has remained largely unchanged since the Reformation in the 16th century.

Today, it is still a church dedicated to regular worship and to the celebration of great events in the life of the nation. Neither a cathedral nor a parish church, Westminster Abbey is a Royal Peculiar under the jurisdiction of a Dean and Chapter, subject only to the sovereign and not to any archbishop or bishop.

Almost every corner tells a story. The Great West façade features ten statues of **Christian martyrs** of the 20th century, including Baptist preacher Martin Luther King. Unveiled in 1998, they are situated in niches that have stood empty since the Middle Ages, and they tower above the figures of Truth, Mercy, Justice and Peace.

The Great West window casts light over the **Nave**, which has the highest medieval Gothic vault in England, at 31 metres (102ft), taking 150 years to build. The weight of the structure is supported by huge flying buttresses. In 1965, 16 splendid Waterford crystal chandeliers were installed to hang in the Nave and transepts of the abbey in order to mark its 900-year anniversary.

The beautiful Henry VII **Lady Chapel** is built in the Perpendicular Gothic style and is the burial place of 15 kings and queens. The elaborate bronze gates are decorated with Tudor badges and the choir stalls were completed in 1512.

The Great West Façade showcases the Christian Martyrs

Edward Blore designed the **Quire** in the mid-19th century in red, blue and gold Victorian Gothic style. It still occupies the same space as the original quire, which was used for worship by the Benedictine monks, and is used regularly today by the Westminster Choir.

The Grave of the Unknown Warrior can be found at the west end of the Nave. The body of a British soldier contained within was brought back from France to be buried in the abbey on the anniversary of Armistice Day, 11 November 1920. The grave, which contains soil from France and is covered by black marble from Belgium, is a moving tribute to those men who died unidentified in the First World War. Part of the inscription on the marble is taken from the Bible and reads: 'they buried him among the Kings'. It is the only tomb set into the floor that you cannot walk over.

The quire inside Westminster Abbey

Upper parts of the North transept and the Rose Window of Westminster Abbey

Buckingham Palace

The official London residence of the UK's sovereigns, Buckingham Palace is a stunning Georgian architectural design built in 1705 as Buckingham House. Since 1837, when Queen Victoria lived here, it has been the home of the royal family. Queen Elizabeth II – or 'Lilibet' to those close to her – resides here with Prince Philip.

Buckingham Palace is still considered a family home, despite being the administrative headquarters of the monarch. The Queen gave birth to Prince Charles and Prince Andrew at the palace and, to this day, the notices of royal births and deaths are attached to the front railings for members of the public to read. The christenings of The Prince of Wales, The Princess Royal, The Duke of York and Prince William took place in the Music Room, and many royal weddings have been celebrated at Buckingham Palace.

Although used for official events and receptions held by The Queen, the State Rooms are open to visitors every year in August and September, when Her Majesty resides at Balmoral Castle in Scotland. The Queen's Gallery is open year-round and the Royal Mews from April to December. The Throne Room's ornate ceiling is illuminated by seven glass and gilt bronze chandeliers that are 200 years old. It is here that The Queen receives addresses on formal occasions.

Around 300 people work at the palace, from officers of the Royal Household to domestic staff. Buckingham Palace has 775 rooms, which include 19 State Rooms, 52 royal and guest bedrooms, 188 staff bedrooms, 92 offices and 78 bathrooms.

Aerial view of Buckingham Palace, with its extensive grounds in the foreground and the Mall beyond.

Built in 1827 for William IV, **Clarence House** was home to the Queen Mother until her death in 2002. She bequeathed it to Prince Charles and he oversaw extensive renovations. Some rooms are now open to the public during the summer for viewing. Displays include the Queen Mother's extensive collection of art and furniture, examples of Fabergé, and English porcelain and silver.

Clarence House, official residence of Charles, Prince of Wales, and Camilla, Duchess of Cornwall.

The **Queen Victoria memorial** was designed in 1901 by Sir Aston Webb and is situated at the entrance to the front of the palace, acting as the centrepiece of the Mall. The seated sculpture created by Sir Thomas Brock is surrounded by symbolic figures representing the Victorian virtues of Truth, Constancy and Courage.

The **Royal Mews** is home to the royal coaches and their horses. The 1761 Gold State Coach, built for George III, and the 1910 Glass Coach, which is used for royal weddings, reside here. The favourite cars of the royal family are also kept and looked after here.

Beautiful vista of the front entrance of Buckingham Palace, closely guarded by the Queen Victorial memorial

An elegant carriage passes Buckingham Palace

Buckingham Palace's balcony is one of the most famous in the world due to its function as a stage. In 1851, Queen Victoria stepped onto the balcony to watch the celebrations to mark the opening of the Great Exhibition. This first recorded royal balcony appearance set a precedent and, since then, royal balcony appearances have marked many occasions, including The Queen's official birthday celebrations, Trooping the Colour and various royal weddings.

The **Queen's Gallery** holds regular themed exhibitions in which it displays the best of the Royal Collection, including old master paintings, drawings by Leonardo da Vinci, textiles, furniture, jewellery and decorative art.

Changing the Guard, known officially as Guard Mounting, takes place every morning between April and July (alternate days during autumn and winter). Visitors can see soldiers in real bearskin hats and red tunics patrolling Buckingham Palace, displaying spectacular military precision. The old guard (Foot Guards of the Household Regiment) comes off duty to be replaced by the new guard on the forecourt of Buckingham Palace.

Changing The Queen's Life Guard takes place every morning by men of the Household Cavalry Mounted Regiment at Horse Guards. Horse Guards is named after the troops who have mounted The Queen's Life Guard since the Restoration of King Charles II in 1660. Members of the Household Cavalry Mounted Regiment ride down from Hyde Park Barracks in Knightsbridge to take over guard duties at 11.00am (Sundays at 10.00am) for the next 24 hours.

Above: Men of the Household Cavalry Mounted Regiment at Horse Guards
Below: Changing the Guard outside Buckingham Palace, the pinnacle of British tradition

The view across St James' Park towards Horse Guards Parade

The magnificent **Trooping the Colour** ceremony takes place on The Queen's official birthday in June. It begins at Buckingham Palace and journeys down the Mall to Horse Guards. This impressive display of pageantry comprises her personal troops, the Household Division, on Horse Guards Parade, with Her Majesty The Queen herself attending and taking the salute. Two hundred horses, over 400 musicians and 1,400 people make up the parade.

Nearby, **St James's Palace** was built by Henry VIII on the site of a former leper hospital. Its impressive gatehouse is one of the most recognisable Tudor sites in London. It contains the London residences of The Princess Royal and Princess Alexandra.

Every year millions of Londoners and tourists visit **St James's Park**, the oldest of the capital's eight royal parks. The park includes the Mall and Horse Guards Parade, and is at the heart of ceremonial London, providing the setting for spectacular pageants including the annual Trooping the Colour. The park offers wonderful views towards Westminster, St James's Palace and Buckingham Palace. The park is also famous for its resident pelicans, which first arrived from Russia as a gift from the ambassador in 1664. The pelicans are fed fresh fish between 2.30pm and 3.00pm daily, and visitors are encouraged to watch. In the summer, there are frequent lunchtime concerts at the bandstand.

A band concert in St James' Park

Trafalgar Square

At the centre of the West End – London's physical, cultural and social heart – Trafalgar Square and the surrounding areas are a sightseeing hub. Trafalgar Square is one of London's busiest areas, and you can enjoy a grand convergence of monumental history, standout entertainment and authentic pubs.

The vista from Trafalgar Square down Whitehall

Trafalgar Square is one of London's great meeting places and was created as a monument to British naval power. The neoclassical design by John Nash provided a dramatic open space and is a gateway for major routes across London. Remodelled in 1840 by Sir Charles Barry, it now includes a number of statues of military and naval heroes. The north side of the square is pedestrianised.

Nelson's column, at the heart of the square, commemorates Nelson's victory over Napoleon in the momentous Battle of Trafalgar in 1805. Curiously, Sir Charles Barry objected to Nelson's column, but was overruled and construction of the imposing 51-metre-high (169ft) column went ahead in 1840, taking three years to build. High above the square, the granite statue of Admiral Lord Nelson stands proudly at the top, looking towards the River Thames and Parliament. At the base, bronze plaques cast from cannons depict scenes from Nelson's battles at St Vincent, the Nile, the bombardment of Copenhagen and also his death at Trafalgar. The lions were added 25 years later.

Trafalgar Square with the Norwegian Christmas tree

The people of Oslo in Norway have donated a **Christmas tree** to Trafalgar Square every year since 1947, as a thank you to Britain for sheltering the Norwegian royal family during the Second World War. The tree-lighting ceremony takes place at the beginning of December, with 770 light bulbs sparkling to the sounds of carol singers.

In the north-eastern corner of Trafalgar Square is the church of **St Martin-in-the-Fields**, the oldest building in the area and once so popular that pews had to be rented. The church, designed by renowned Scottish architect James Gibbs, was completed in 1726 and was so named because the area was beyond the city boundaries and surrounded by green fields.

Nelson's Column in Trafalgar Square with the National Gallery behind

COVENT GARDEN

Covent Garden was once a market garden used by medieval monks from Westminster Abbey and later became renowned as London's main fruit and vegetable centre. In 1974, the market moved to Nine Elms at Vauxhall and the buildings were modernised to provide specialist shops selling crafts, jewellery and clothing. The piazza in front of St Paul's Church, known as The Actors' Church, has an abundance of street theatre, from knife jugglers, fire swallowers and unicyclists to string quartets and Punch and Judy shows. On the opposite side of the square is London's Transport Museum.

View of Trafalgar Square with St Martin-in-the-Fields church in the background

Charles II's mistress, Nell Gwynne, was buried here but the crypt was cleared and used as an air-raid shelter during the Second World War.

On the north side of Trafalgar Square is the magnificent **National Gallery**, containing one of the most extensive painting collections in the world. With more than 2,000 Western European paintings on display, this is one of the largest galleries in the world, although it is the quality rather than the quantity of the works that impresses most. There are seminal paintings from every important epoch in the history of art, from the mid-13th to the early 20th centuries, by artists such as Leonardo da Vinci, Michelangelo, Titian, Van Gogh, Monet and Renoir.

One of the lions guarding Nelson's Column, with the National Gallery in the background

The **National Portrait Gallery**, in St Martin's Place, contains more than 10,000 portraits of the best-known faces in Britain, from politicians and sportsmen to writers and heroes. There is a cartoon of Henry VIII and paintings of his wives, along with the earliest portrait of Shakespeare, and Horatio Nelson together with his mistress, Emma Hamilton. The rooftop restaurant has wonderful views over Trafalgar Square and Whitehall.

Close by is the beautiful 18th-century **Somerset House**, originally used as government offices and now the home of the Courtauld Institute Gallery, which has a fine art collection. From November until January the central courtyard is transformed into a magnificent outdoor ice-skating rink, adorned with a Christmas tree – which must be exactly 12 metres (40ft) tall – that is presided over by a Christmas tree curator.

Winter ice skating at Somerset House

Piccadilly Circus and Soho

London's Theatreland offers a cornucopia of plays, musicals and concerts. A night out in the West End is an experience not to be missed! The Shaftesbury Memorial Fountain is found at the southeastern side of Piccadilly Circus. The statue depicts a winged, nude figure, commonly mistaken for Eros. It has been called London's most famous work of sculpture.

London's cosmopolitan **West End** offers a lively mixture of social activities, with pubs, clubs, shopping, theatres, wine bars and cafes. Be sure to catch the street performers including talented dancers, singers and jugglers, and look up to see the huge lit-up video billboards. World-famous Oxford Street is over a mile long and includes huge department stores such as **Selfridges**. This shopper's delight stretches from Marble Arch to Tottenham Court Road.

London's busy **Theatreland** centres along the streets of Haymarket and Shaftesbury Avenue, and offers productions of the latest dramas, musicals and comedies. There are also many cafes, bars and restaurants to visit before or after the shows.

Regent Street is home to many popular stores such as **Hamley's**, one of the largest toy shops in the world. Behind these stores is the famous 1960s hippy haunt of **Carnaby Street**, now a paved walkway where well-known shops blend with bohemian emporiums that sell everything from posters to hand-made jewellery.

Christmas lights in the West End

Shaftesbury Avenue, the heart of Theatreland

To the south of Bond Street, situated on Piccadilly, lies **Burlington Arcade**, a shopping precinct dating from 1819. It retains much of its unique character and is still an historical experience, with Edwardian-frocked Burlington Beadles in top hats enforcing Regency law to ensure no one runs or whistles.

Leicester Square is a throng of activity, illuminated at night by the multiplex cinemas bordering the central garden, which contains statues of playwright William Shakespeare and comedian Charlie Chaplin.

To the south of Shaftesbury Avenue is London's **Chinatown**, which offers a wide choice of excellent restaurants. The street signs are in English and Chinese, and Chinese archways span each end of Gerrard Street. Every January or February the Chinese New Year is celebrated with demonstrations of traditional music and dance, and a beautiful display of hanging lanterns in the streets.

The Ritz is a name synonymous with luxury and this iconic hotel commands a landmark position in the heart of London. Afternoon tea is something of a British tradition here, with bars and restaurants aplenty.

With its classic turquoise colour scheme, London's oldest grocery store, **Fortnum & Mason**, is a beautiful shopping and restaurant experience in one, with an elegant wine bar nestled within the famous Food Hall.

Fortnum & Mason in Piccadilly

A colourful Chinese arch in Gerrard Street

17

Kensington and Knightsbridge

Kensington is sightseeing land at its best. The grand museums in London are found here, many transforming their outdoor spaces into ice-skating rinks and Christmas markets during the winter season.

A vast array of ceramics, furniture, fashion, glass, jewellery, metalwork, photographs, sculpture, textiles and paintings make the **Victoria and Albert Museum** one of the world's greatest art and design museums, with miles of galleries to explore. The breadth and depth of the collection is staggering, from Chinese ceramics to Islamic textiles.

The **Royal Albert Hall**, with its iron and glass roof, was designed by engineer Francis Fowke. Inspired by Roman amphitheatres, it was completed in 1871. The colourful Promenade Concerts (Proms) take place here every summer.

With its animatronic T-Rex, earthquake simulator, Wildlife Garden and Gothic fairytale architecture, the **Natural History Museum** is a work of great curatorial imagination. The nearby **Science Museum** covers everything from early technology to space travel arranged over seven floors of interactive exhibits.

The Serpentine lake in Hyde Park

The Royal Albert Hall, home to the Proms every summer

A statue of Queen Victoria stands in front of Kensington Palace

The famous Harrods store in Knightsbridge

Kensington Gardens offer tree-lined avenues, a flower walk, roller-blading paths and model yachts on the Round Pond. The Serpentine Gallery, housed in a 1934 tea pavilion, is home to contemporary art and architectural displays, and marks the start of the Diana, Princess of Wales memorial walk.

Kensington Palace was the royal residence of Princess Diana for over 15 years and a public exhibition at the palace celebrates her life. Now, the palace is home to Prince William and Catherine, the Duke and Duchess of Cambridge, and their children. Prince Harry lives in separate quarters within the palace.

During the Dissolution of the Monasteries in 1536, Henry VIII used **Hyde Park** for hunting. Today visitors can boat, swim and listen to debates at Speakers' Corner. During the summer, concerts are held and traditional gun salutes, marking state occasions, are fired from the parade ground.

Harrods is a must-see for the Food Hall, the Egyptian Elevator and the memorial fountain to Dodi Fayed and Princess Diana, not to mention the huge array of goods to browse.

South Bank

The South Bank boasts riverside sights such as the cultural enclave of the Southbank Centre and Tate Modern, Millennium Bridge, Shakespeare's Globe, waterside pubs, a cathedral and one of London's most visited food markets, with skateboarders and street entertainers lining the walkways. At Christmas, it transforms into a magical festive market with gingerbread stalls and carol singing.

Around six million visitors flock to the **Tate Modern** each year. Housed in a former power station, this modern-art collection enjoys a triumphant position on the Thames.

Close to London Bridge Station is the **Shard**, opened to the public in 2013. At 309.7 metres (1,016ft), it is the tallest building in the United Kingdom.

Also on the riverside are two key London attractions. The **Sea Life London Aquarium** has around 3,500 species on show with a one-million-litre water tank and **London Dungeon** offers a scary experience with ghostly boat rides and actors dressed up as torturers and criminals, including Jack the Ripper and Sweeney Todd.

The original 1599 **Shakespeare's Globe** was known as the Wooden O after its circular shape and roofless centre. The theatre burned to the ground in less than two hours during a performance in 1613, after a stage cannon ignited the thatched roof. The new Globe was designed to resemble the original, with the arena open to the London skies.

Shakespeare's Globe and Tate Modern stand side by side on Bankside

The Imperial War Museum

Painstakingly constructed with 600 oak pegs, specially fired Tudor bricks and thatching reeds from Norfolk, even the plaster contains goat hair, lime and sand as it did in Shakespeare's time.

In existence since the 13th century, 'London's Larder' **Borough Market** overflows with food lovers. This fantastic market has become firmly established as a sight in its own right, specialising in high-end fresh produce with plenty of takeaway stalls, free tastings and a vast array of cakes.

The fascinating **Imperial War Museum** is housed in what used to be Bethlem Royal Hospital, also known as Bedlam. Through a variety of exhibitions it tells the stories of people's experiences of war from the First World War to the present day. Permanent displays include the First World War Galleries and The Holocaust Exhibition.

The **Old Operating Theatre Museum** is Britain's oldest operating theatre. Climb the 32 steps in the 1703 tower of St Thomas's Church and look back at the horror of 19th-century surgery.

The Shard at London Bridge has a viewing platform offering amazing views of London

British Museum

The British Museum is dedicated to documenting the story of human existence, art and culture. You'll find the magestic building at the heart of the Bloomsbury area of London. The permanent collection holds 8 million works and is among the largest and most comprehensive in existence

The stunning modern roof over the Great Court of the British Museum

Founded in 1753 as the first national public museum in the world, the **British Museum** contains the largest collection of treasures in Britain and welcomes more than six million visitors each year. With free entry and open nearly every day of the year, the British Museum is an inspiring and educational place to visit, with galleries documenting human history and traditions worldwide.

With a range of both permanent and temporary exhibitions, visitors can step back in time and visit the ancient world and delve into cultures long-since forgotten.

The museum's most famous objects are the Elgin Marbles from the Parthenon in Athens, the Rosetta Stone, which helped decipher Egyptian hieroglyphs, the 12th century Lewis chess pieces from the Outer Hebrides, and the vast collection of Egyptian mummies. The collections also include Roman art and sculpture from Britain, the Sutton Hoo ship burial from Suffolk, Chinese bronzes and a large collection of prints and watercolours.

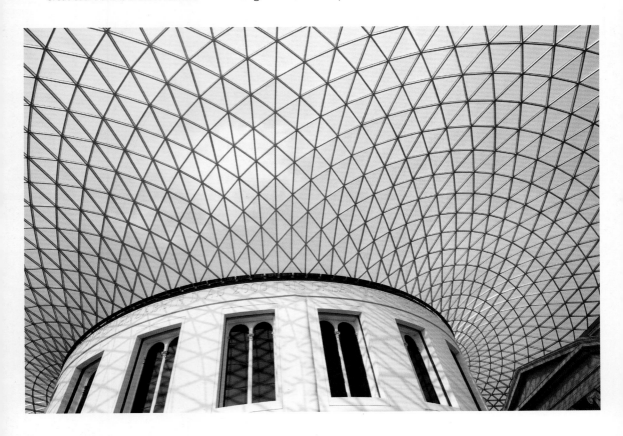

Aerial view of the British Museum

The pediment over the entrance to the British Museum has sculptures representing the Progress of Civilisation

Bloomsbury

Historically, Bloomsbury is associated with the arts, literature, education and medicine. Home to the British Museum, the British Library, universities, traditional taverns and leafy Georgian squares, Bloomsbury is delightfully charming.

Tucked into a corner of the Borough of Camden, the Bloomsbury area is an intellectual playground. It boasts some of the most prestigious school and colleges in the United Kingdom and luminaries of the written word, such as Virginia Woolf, T.S. Eliot, Charles Dickens and George Bernard Shaw, have all left their mark.

The **British Library** is the second largest library in the world. It spans 3,000 years and contains more than 150 million items representing every age of written civilisation dating back to 2000 BC. It houses some fascinating and treasured manuscripts, including 14 million books. Every year it increases it's collection by 3 million items, occupying 6 miles (10 km) of new shelf space.

The **Wellcome Collection** is a clever and intriguing museum that explores the relationships between medicine, art and life through the ages. There is a library, interactive displays and changing exhibitions inspired by the history of medicine.

Aerial shot of the British Library at St Pancras

St Pancras Station and the Renaissance Hotel are among London's finest Victorian Gothic buildings

St Pancras Station and the **St Pancras Renaissance Hotel** have been restored to their former 19th-century glory. The station features a fascinating 9-metre-tall (29ft) bronze statue of two lovers and hosts a regular food market. The hotel is situated within a beautiful building and offers a glamorous experience reminiscent of Victorian times.

Next door in King's Cross Station, visitors can view Platform 9¾, a photo opportnity not to be missed by any **Harry Potter** fan.

One of Britain's leading authors, Charles Dickens, resided at 48 Doughty Street from 1837 to 1839, and the house has now been converted into the **Charles Dickens Museum**. Visitors can see the desk where he worked, imagine how he entertained his many guests at dinner, and be captivated by the letters, stories and novels that he wrote.

Charles Dickens Museum at 48 Doughty Street

Tower Bridge

Tower Bridge has been a beloved symbol of modern London for 120 years. It is a tourist attraction, events venue and listed heritage site, with glass walkways that make it more interactive than ever before.

Tower Bridge has been standing at its location, guarding the access to the old Pool of London with its docks and warehouses, since 1894. Its ancient-looking façade is deceptive and at least partly due to royal objection. Her Majesty Queen Victoria was not amused when faced with the prospect of having a modern steel structure erected next to the venerable Tower of London. What now looks like something from a medieval fairy tale is, underneath its crenellations, dragon sculptures, turrets and golden crown, a marvel of 19th-century English engineering.

It is a sophisticated steel structure held up by piers, which were sunk ten metres into the river with the help of a crew of Victorian divers. The bridge was built with the ability to split apart and rise up to allow river traffic to pass beneath it – a feat that still takes place today. Huge pumping engines powered by steam performed this task until 1976, when the steam was replaced by oil and electricity. The original steam engines, furnaces and accumulators can now be found in the magnificent Victorian **Engine Rooms**, located a short walk from the South Tower.

Tower Bridge is the iconic symbol of London

The golden fiery urn on top of the Monument

Upriver from Tower Bridge is **The Monument**, designed by Sir Christopher Wren and Robert Hooke, and stands 62 metres (202ft) high. Adjacent to busy London Bridge, dwarfed by the neighbouring high-rise office blocks and surrounded by pubs and shops on the City of London's southern reach, it commemorates the Great Fire of 1666 that almost destroyed London. It engulfed the city for four days and nights, devastating a significant area.

Wren designed the column in the Doric style and located it 62 metres (202ft) from the bakery on Pudding Lane where the fire broke out. The inscriptions on its base are in Latin and describe the fire and the rebuilding of London. It is crowned with an elaborate representation of the fire in gilded metal, and from meshed cage, which circles the top. Visitors who climb the 311 steps are rewarded with a marvellous view over the ever-changing landscape of the city.

The Monument was built to commemorate the Great Fire of 1666

Tower of London

The Tower of London's imposing stone fortress is well known for its grisly history, having served as a jail and execution site for many years. With a history as bleak and bloody as it is fascinating, the Tower of London is one of London's must-see sights.

Begun during the reign of William the Conqueror (1066–87), the **Tower of London** is actually a castle and has served through history as a palace, observatory, storehouse and mint. Today, it is home to the dazzling Crown Jewels, rumoured to be worth £20 billion. A travelator conveys you past the centrepiece crowns, which include the Imperial State Crown – set with 2,868 diamonds, plus sapphires, emeralds, rubies and pearls – and the platinum-framed Queen Elizabeth The Queen Mother's Crown, famously set with the 106-carat Koh-i-Noor (Mountain of Light) diamond.

Yeoman Warders have been guarding the tower since the late 15th century and in order to be appointed, they must have first served a minimum of 22 years in any branch of the British Armed Forces. They live within the tower walls and are known affectionately as Beefeaters, a name they dislike. The origin of the name is unknown, although it is thought to be due to their entitlement to consume large rations of beef from the king's table.

Aerial view of the Tower of London

The White Tower at the heart of the Tower of London

Legend has it that Charles II requested that ravens should always be kept at the Tower, believing the kingdom would fall apart if they left. There are usually at least six ravens at the Tower and their wings are clipped to placate the superstitious.

Begun in 1078, the **White Tower** was the original Tower of London, built as a palace and fortress. By modern standards it is not tall, but in the Middle Ages it would have dwarfed the surrounding huts of the peasantry. Inside, along with St John's Chapel, the tower has retained some remnants of Norman architecture, including a fireplace and garderobe (lavatory).

The **Bloody Tower** takes its nickname from when the Princes in the Tower – Edward V and his younger brother Richard – were held here during Richard III's reign and then vanished mysteriously. An exhibition allows the visitor to vote on who they think was responsible for their disappearance. There are also exhibits on Sir Walter Raleigh, who was imprisoned here three times.

Traitors's Gate, through which many prisoners arrived at the Tower of London

View of the City from the Thames, with many of the modern high-rise structures alongside older buildings. The 'Walkie Talkie' is in the centre, and the 'Gherkin' is far right.

St Paul's Cathedral

St Paul's Cathedral dominates London's skyline and has done so for over 300 years. Sir Christopher Wren's baroque architectural wonder is fascinating inside and out. Climb 111 metres (364ft) above London to the dome's Golden Gallery for sweeping 360-degree panoramic views or go underground and discover the Crypt.

St Paul's Cathedral

The first view that visitors encounter is the breathtaking vista of the cathedral floor stretching all the way along the Nave. The Great West Doors at the end of the Nave stand nine metres (29ft) tall and are used only for special services and the arrival of visitors such as The Queen and the Lord Mayor of London.

Rather than a spire atop **St Paul's Cathedral**, Wren insisted upon a dome. Unusual in England in the late 17th century, the dome is one of the largest in the world, weighing 65,000 tonnes and comprising the Golden Gallery, the Whispering Gallery and the Stone Gallery. A ball and cross can be found at its highest point. Despite being in his seventies, during construction Wren was raised up and down the three-dome structure in a basket to check on progress.

Dating from 1958, the magnificent High Altar is made of marble and carved and gilded oak. It replaces a large Victorian marble altar, which was damaged in the Blitz along with a large section of the eastern end of the cathedral.

St Paul's Cathedral still dominates the London skyline

The **Whispering Gallery** can be reached via 257 steps from the cathedral floor. A quirk in its construction means that a whisper against its walls can be heard on the opposite side.

The **Crypt** houses the tombs of Lord Nelson, the Duke of Wellington and Sir Christopher Wren. The simple stone that marks Wren's tomb sits underneath the Latin epitaph that famously addresses the visitor: 'Reader, if you seek his monument, look around you.' There are many tombs and memorials of artists, scientists and musicians within the Crypt, including scientist Alexander Fleming, who discovered penicillin, and the sculptor Henry Moore. Moore's evocative sculpture **Mother and Child** can be found in the north Quire aisle.

Charles and Diana, the Prince and Princess of Wales, were married in the cathedral in 1981 and the wedding was broadcast live to an estimated global television audience of 750 million; two million spectators lined the route of Diana's procession into the City.

In 1965, former British Prime Minister Sir Winston Churchill's funeral was held in the cathedral and, in 2013, that of Baroness Margaret Thatcher.

The Square Mile

The Square Mile is London's financial district, home to landmarks such as the Stock Exchange, Mansion House and the Bank of England. Explore beneath the surface of the Square Mile and discover 2,000 years of London's history, from Roman ruins to art, treasures and curiosities collected over the centuries.

This area is home to London's 110 most ancient and modern trade associations and guilds, the livery companies of the City of London. The annual **Lord Mayor's Show** – over 800 years old – is regarded as a classic piece of British pageantry. The Lord Mayor arrives in the City by river amid a splendid flotilla of traditional Thames barges and small boats, including the famous QRB *Gloriana*. The procession then continues by road with the Lord Mayor seated in the magnificent State Coach and the day culminates in a spectacular fireworks finale.

Designed by the architects Chamberlin, Powell and Bon, and officially opened by Queen Elizabeth II, the **Barbican Centre** is a large arts complex that houses a theatre, art gallery, cinemas, concert hall and library.

Guildhall Art Gallery has works dating back to 1670, including Victorian and Pre-Raphaelite masterpieces. Established in 1886 as 'a Collection of Art Treasures worthy of the capital city', the visitor can view 17th-century portraits and a range of paintings documenting London's dramatic history. Underneath the Guildhall

The Lord Mayor greets the crowds during the Lord Mayor's Show

The ancient Guildhall in the City of London

Art Gallery is **London's Roman Amphitheatre**, dating from AD 70. Beautifully lit, it transports you back in time to when it was used as a venue for gladiatorial combat in order to entertain the populace.

The magnificent **Guildhall Great Hall**, measuring 46 metres (152ft) long, is second in size only to Westminster Hall. Despite being partially burnt in the Great Fire of 1666, and bombed in the Second World War, much of the medieval fabric survives to this day.

Guildhall Library is the oldest public reference library in the UK, specialising in the history of London. The collection comprises over 200,000 titles, including Shakespeare's First Folio, a 13th-century bible and historic British Parliamentary papers. Designed by Sir Horace Jones, **Leadenhall Market** is a magnificent Victorian temple to retail, with a beautifully ornate iron roof and cobbled streets. Its striking appearance makes it a popular film location, including as Diagon Alley in the Harry Potter films. In November the Christmas lights are switched on by the Lord Mayor of the City of London. Beneath the curious cobbled pathways of the Square Mile lies a rich Roman history that has survived 2,000 years of building works, fires and bombings. Lower Thames Street is home to one of Roman London's most fascinating remains: the **Billingsgate Roman Bathhouse**. The site was discovered in 1848 and is now open to the public.

One of the two mythical giants called Gog and Magog, traditionally guardians of the City, that are housed in the Guildhall

Regent's Park and Camden

Regent's Park, Camden Market and Hampstead Heath are all worth visiting. Camden is a buzzing place situated by the canal, while Regent's Park is an oasis of calm and home to London Zoo. Hampstead Heath offers a slice of the countryside and on Baker Street you can meet Sherlock Holmes.

Sherlock Holmes solved many mysteries from his residence at 221b Baker Street, as told by the author Sir Arthur Conan Doyle. **The Sherlock Holmes Museum** faithfully recreates his beautiful Victorian home.

At **Madame Tussauds** visitors can meet and take photographs of the most famous wax faces in the world, from movie stars to royalty.

Designed in 1811 by John Nash for the Prince Regent, **Regent's Park** contains a private residential estate, Queen Mary's Gardens, a lake and a heronry and waterfowl collection. It is also home to the famous **London Zoo**, which hosts over 700 species of animal, has a penguin beach and lodges where you can stay overnight next to the lions.

Hampstead Heath is one of London's most popular open spaces, situated just six kilometres (3.7 miles) from the city centre. The magic of the Heath lies not only in its rich wildlife and extensive sports and recreational opportunities, but also in its accessibility for millions of people. There is a small zoo, an athletics track, an education centre, three swimming ponds and a lido. Traverse

Opposite top right: The lake in Regent's Park, with the London Central Mosque over the trees
Below: The Sherlock Holmes Museum in Baker Street

Left: Keats House in Hampstead, now a museum

Right: Narrowboats on the Regent's Canal

the Heath to the magnificent neoclassical 18th-century **Kenwood House** in a glorious sweep of perfectly landscaped gardens leading down to a picturesque lake. The house contains a magnificent collection of art, including paintings by Rembrandt, Constable and Turner.

At the Heath's edge is a marvellous 1585 tavern once visited by literary greats such as Byron, Shelley, Keats and Dickens. A former toll house, the **Spaniard's Inn** has kept much of its historic charm.

Discover the beauty of poetry and place in the home of the Romantic poet John Keats, now a museum and literary centre. Explore the life and work of Keats through original manuscripts and other artefacts. **Keats House** comes alive with special events throughout the year, from poetry performances to family fun days.

The canals that were once a trade lifeline for the capital have become a favourite escape for Londoners. It is possible to walk along Regent's Canal from **Little Venice** to Camden in under an hour. There are dozens of food stalls at the Camden Lock Market as well as many trendy fashion shops.

Greenwich and The Royal Observatory

Greenwich is home to an unrivalled array of beautiful classical buildings lining the banks of the River Thames. There you can straddle the Meridian Line – the reference line that divides the earth's eastern and western hemispheres.

The Queen's House in Greenwich, which was built by Inigo Jones

Great architects of the Enlightenment made their mark here. Charles II was a great admirer of the area, commissioning Sir Christopher Wren to build both the Royal Observatory and part of the Royal Naval College.

The **Royal Observatory** allows for a fascinating exploration of the mysteries of time and space, and showcases the endeavours of astronomers in placing Greenwich at the centre of the world, with the creation of Greenwich Mean Time.

The Peter Harrison **Planetarium** – the only one in London – transports you into distant galaxies, flies you to the heart of the sun and lands you on Mars. The wonders of the night sky are regularly brought to life by expert commentaries from astronomers.

In the **Meridian Courtyard** it is possible to straddle the eastern and western hemispheres of the earth by placing one foot either side of the Prime Meridian line. Each evening at dusk, the position of the Meridian Line is marked by a green laser in the sky, stretching out from the hill in Greenwich Park across the London skyline.

The Peter Harrison Planetarium

THE O2

The iconic dome-shaped structure was built in 1999 to celebrate the start of the third millennium. It was originally known as the Millennium Dome and housed the Millennium Experience, a major exhibition. In 2007 it was reopened as the O2 Arena and now houses The O2 Entertainment Avenue and arena. Visitors can now Climb to the top of the dome.

The **Cutty Sark** was the last of the great clipper ships to sail between China and England in the 19th century. It has been restored and is now displayed in a very modern way. The exhibition in the ship's hold tells her story.

The **National Maritime Museum** holds the world's largest maritime collection, with ten free galleries containing art, maps, manuscripts and thousands of other objects. The sculpture of 'Nelson's Ship in a Bottle' is one of the most photographed sculptures in London.

The **Old Royal Naval College** is a magnificent example of classical architecture. You can visit the Chapel of St Peter and St Paul, a neoclassical masterpiece that boasts one of the finest 18th-century interiors in the UK, and enjoy some of the best views over London.

Greenwich Park is one of London's eight royal parks. It has a rose garden, picturesque walks and offers wonderful views from the top of the hill, across the River Thames all the way to St Paul's Cathedral. The park is also home to The Wilderness, a deer park where visitors are invited to view these magnificent animals from several designated viewing areas.

The Cutty Sark in dry dock at Greenwich

Around London

To the west, London borders Berkshire, where The Queen has her second home; further afield is the 500-year-old Hampton Court Palace, which is home to the last surviving royal chocolate kitchen; and in Kew the visitor can discover London's celebrated botanic gardens.

A residence of British royalty for over 900 years, **Windsor Castle** is the oldest and largest inhabited castle in the world. Originally built from wood by William the Conqueror in 1070, it was intended to guard the western approaches to the capital. The magnificent State Apartments showcase some of the finest works of art from the Royal Collection, and St George's Chapel holds the tombs of ten sovereigns. The Queen and the royal family spend most of their private weekends at Windsor, when The Royal Standard flies from the Round Tower, and the castle is also used for official and ceremonial occasions.

Windsor Great Park spans 4,800 acres and at one time was popular with Saxon kings as a hunting forest. It is said the ghost of Herne – King Richard II's favourite huntsman – still appears wearing stag antlers and riding a phantom black stallion at the head of a pack of black hounds.

Hampton Court Palace is London's most spectacular Tudor palace. Steeped in British history, it boasts Tudor architecture and rooms designed by Wren. It is surrounded by gorgeous landscaped gardens,

Aerial view of Windsor Castle

Aerial view of Hampton Court Palace, with its Tudor gatehouse

and you can get lost in the 800-metre-long (2,625ft) maze. In 1515 Cardinal Thomas Wolsey, Lord Chancellor of England, built the palace for himself but later presented it to Henry VIII.

Henry set to work expanding it, adding the Great Hall, the exquisite Chapel Royal and the sprawling kitchens. By 1540 it had become one of the grandest and most sophisticated palaces in Europe. Henry's fifth wife, Catherine Howard, was arrested for adultery and detained in the palace in 1542. She was dragged screaming down a gallery by her guards after a failed escape attempt. To this day, her ghost is said to repeat the performance in the **Haunted Gallery**.

In 1759, King George III's mother created **Kew Gardens** on a nine-acre site. The Royal Botanic Gardens were presented to the nation in 1841 and now feature over 40,000 species of plants. There are world-class attractions to enjoy, from iconic buildings and glasshouses to inspirational gardens and landscapes. The Princess of Wales Conservatory features ten climate zones and hosts Madagascan baobab trees, orchids from Central America and carnivorous plants from Asia.

View of Kew Gardens, with its famous pagoda

Essential Information

Most places of interest are open throughout the year, but closed on Christmas Day, Boxing Day and certain Bank Holidays. Please check for details on these days.
* Nearest London Transport Underground Station
# Nearest British Rail Station

Bank of England Museum
Bartholomew Lane, EC2R 8AH
Tel: 020 7601 5545
www.bankofengland.co.uk/museum
* Bank / Docklands Light Railway

Banqueting House
Whitehall, SW1A 2ER
Tel: 020 3166 6000
www.hrp.org.uk/banqueting-house
* Westminster

Barbican Centre
Silk Street, EC2Y 8DS
Tel: 020 7638 8891
www.barbican.org.uk
*# Barbican

Billingsgate Roman House & Baths
101 Lower Thames St, EC3R 6DL
Tel: 020 7001 9844
www.cityoflondon.gov.uk/romanbathhouse
* Monument/Tower Hill

Borough Market
8 Southwark Street, SE1 1TL
Tel: 020 7407 1002
boroughmarket.org.uk
*# London Bridge

British Library
96 Euston Road, NW1 2DB
Tel: 0330 333 1144
www.bl.uk
*# Euston/King's Cross/
* Euston Square

British Museum
Great Russell Street, WC1B 3DG
Tel: 020 7323 8299
www.britishmuseum.org
* Tottenham Court Rd/Russell Square

Buckingham Palace
The State Rooms, Buckingham Palace, SW1A 1AA
Tel: 0303 123 7300
www.royalcollection.org.uk/visit/the-state-rooms-buckingham-palace
* St James's Park/Green Park/
*# Victoria

Burlington Arcade
51 Piccadilly, W1J 0QJ
Tel: 020 7493 1764
www.burlingtonarcade.com
* Green Park/Piccadilly Circus

Changing the Guard Ceremony
Buckingham Palace: Apr – end July: daily at 11.30am
Alternate days remainder of year
www.royalcollection.org.uk/visit/buckinghampalace/what-to-see-and-do/changing-the-guard
* St James's Park/Green Park/
*# Victoria
Horse Guards, Whitehall: daily, Mon–Sat 11.00am, Sun 10.00am
* Westminster/ *# Charing Cross

Charles Dickens Museum
48 Doughty Street, WC1N 2LX
Tel: 020 7405 2127
www.dickensmuseum.com
* Russell Square/Chancery Lane

Churchill War Rooms
Clive Steps, King Charles Street, SW1A 2AQ
Tel: 020 7930 6961
www.iwm.org.uk/visits/churchill-war-rooms
* Westminster/St James's Park

City of London Police Museum
Enter via Guildhall Library, Aldermanbury, EC2V 7HH
Tel: 020 7332 1868
www.cityoflondon.gov.uk/guildhallgalleries
* Bank/St Paul's/Mansion House/*# Moorgate

Courtauld Institute of Art Gallery
Somerset House, Strand, WC2R 0RN
Tel: 020 7848 2526
courtauld.ac.uk/gallery
* Temple/Covent Garden

Covent Garden
www.coventgarden.london
* Covent Garden

Cutty Sark
King William Walk, Greenwich, SE10 9HT
Tel: 020 8312 6608
www.rmg.co.uk/cutty-sark
Cutty Sark (DLR), Greenwich/Maze Hill or boat from Westminster, Charing Cross or Tower Hill to Greenwich Pier

Dennis Severs' House
18 Folgate St, E1 6BX
Tel: 020 7247 4013
www.dennissevershouse.co.uk
*# Liverpool Street/# Shoreditch High Street

Dr Johnson's House
17 Gough Square, EC4A 3DE
Tel: 020 7353 3745
www.drjohnsonshouse.org
* Chancery Lane/Temple/*#Blackfriars/Farringdon/#City Thameslink

The Geffrye Museum of the Home
136 Kingsland Road, E2 8EA
Tel: 020 7739 9893
www.geffrye-museum.org.uk
Hoxton/ * Old Street

Guildhall Art Gallery & London's Roman Amphitheatre
Guildhall Yard, EC2V 5AE
Tel: 020 7332 3700
www.cityoflondon.gov.uk/guildhallgalleries
* Bank/St Paul's/Mansion House/ *# Moorgate

Guildhall Great Hall
Gresham St, EC2V 5AE
Tel: 020 7332 3700
www.cityoflondon.gov.uk/guildhallgalleries
* Bank/St Paul's/Mansion House/Moorgate

Hampton Court Palace
East Molesey, Surrey, KT8 9AU
Tel: 020 3166 6000
www.hrp.org.uk/hampton-court-palace
Hampton Court

Harrods
87–135 Brompton Road, Knightsbridge, SW1X 7XL
Tel: 020 3626 7020
www.harrods.com
* Knightsbridge

Hayward Gallery
Southbank Centre, Belvedere Road, SE1 8XX
Tel: 020 7960 4200
www.southbankcentre.co.uk/venues/hayward-gallery
*# Waterloo

HMS Belfast
The Queen's Walk, SE1 2JH
Tel: 020 7940 6300
www.iwm.org.uk/visits/hms-belfast
*# London Bridge; ferry from Tower Pier

Houses of Parliament
Parliament Square, SW1A 0AA
Tel: 020 7219 4114
www.parliament.uk/visiting
* Westminster

Imperial War Museum
Lambeth Road, SE1 6HZ
Tel: 020 7416 5000
www.iwm.org.uk/visits/iwm-london
* Lambeth North/Elephant & Castle/Southwark

Sir John Soane's Museum
13 Lincoln's Inn Fields, WC2A 3BP
Tel: 020 7405 2107
www.soane.org
* Holborn/Temple

Keats House
10 Keats Grove, Hampstead, NW3 2RR
Tel: 020 7332 3868
www.keatshouse.org.uk
Hampstead Heath/* Hampstead/Belsize Park

Kensington Palace State Apartments
Kensington Gardens, W8 4PX
Tel: 020 3166 6000
www.hrp.org.uk/kensington-palace
* High Street Kensington

Kenwood House
Hampstead Lane, NW3 7JR
Tel: 0370 333 1181
www.english-heritage.org.uk/visit/places/kenwood/
Gospel Oak/Hampstead Heath

Kew Garden (Royal Botanic Gardens)
Kew, Richmond, Surrey, TW9 3AB
Tel: 0844 995 9672
www.kew.org
Kew Gardens

London Dungeon
County Hall, Westminster Bridge Road, SE1 7PB
www.thedungeons.com/london
 # Waterloo/ Westminster

London Eye
Riverside Building, County Hall, Westminster Bridge Road, SE1 7PB
www.londoneye.com
* Embankment/Westminster/ *# Waterloo

London Zoo
ZSL London Zoo, Regent's Park, NW1 4RY
Tel: 0344 225 1826
www.londonzoo.co.uk
* Regent's Park/Camden Town

Madame Tussaud's
Marylebone Road, NW1 5LR
www.madametussauds.com/london
* Baker Street

Monument
Fish St Hill, London, EC3R 8AH
Tel: 020 7403 3761
http://www.themonument.org.
uk/
* Monument

Museum in Docklands
No 1 Warehouse, West India
Quay, E14 4AL
Tel: 020 7001 9844
www.museumoflondon.org.uk/
museum-london-docklands
* Canary Wharf

Museum of London
150 London Wall, EC2Y 5HN
Tel: 020 7001 9844
www.museumoflondon.org.uk
*# Barbican/ * St Paul's

National Gallery
Trafalgar Square, WC2N 5DN
Tel: 020 7747 2885
www.nationalgallery.org.uk
*# Charing Cross/ * Leicester
Square

National Maritime Museum
Romney Road, Greenwich,
London SE10 9NF
Tel: 020 8312 6565
www.rmg.co.uk/national-
maritime-museum
Cutty Sark/Greenwich/Maze
Hill or boat from Westminster,
Charing Cross and Tower Pier to
Greenwich Pier

Natural History Museum
Cromwell Road, SW7 5BD
Tel: 020 7942 5000
www.nhm.ac.uk
* South Kensington

National Portrait Gallery
St Martin's Place, WC2H 0HE
Tel: 020 7306 0055
www.npg.org.uk
*# Charing Cross/ * Leicester
Square

The Queen's Gallery
Buckingham Palace, SW1A 1AA
Tel: 0303 123 7301
www.royalcollection.org.uk/
visit/the-queens-gallery-
buckingham-palace
*# Victoria/ * St James's Park/
Green Park

The Ritz
150 Piccadilly, W1J 9BR
Tel: 020 7493 8181
www.theritzlondon.com
* Green Park

Royal Academy of Arts
Burlington House, Piccadilly,
W1J 0BD
Tel: 020 7300 8000
www.royalacademy.org.uk
* Piccadilly Circus/Green Park

Royal Albert Hall
Kensington Gore, SW7 2AP
Tel: 020 7589 8212
www.royalalberthall.com
* South Kensington/High Street
Kensington

Royal Festival Hall
Southbank Centre, Belvedere
Road, SE1 8XX
Tel: 0207 960 4200
www.rfh.org.uk
*# Waterloo

Royal Mews
Buckingham Palace, SW1W 0QH
Tel: 0303 123 7302
www.royalcollection.org.uk/visit/
royalmews
 # Victoria/ Green Park

Royal Observatory
Romney Road, Greenwich,
London SE10 9NF
Tel: 020 8312 6565
www.rmg.co.uk/royal-
observatory
Cutty Sark/Greenwich/Maze
Hill or boat from Westminster,
Charing Cross and Tower Pier to
Greenwich Pier

Royal Opera House
Bow Street, Covent Garden,
WC2E 9DD
Tel: 020 7304 4000
www.roh.org.uk
* Covent Garden

St Paul's Cathedral
St Paul's Churchyard, EC4M 8AD
Tel: 0207 246 8350
www.stpauls.co.uk
* St Paul's/Mansion House

Science Museum
Exhibition Road, South
Kensington, SW7 2DD.
Tel: 020 7942 4000
www.sciencemuseum.org.uk
* South Kensington

Sea Life London Aquarium
County Hall, Westminster Bridge
Road, SE1 7PB
www.visitsealife.com/london
*# Waterloo/ * Westminster

Shakespeare's Globe Theatre
21 New Globe Walk, Bankside,
SE1 9DT
Tel: 020 7902 1400
www.shakespearesglobe.com
* Southwark/London Bridge/
Mansion House/ # London
Bridge

Sherlock Holmes Museum
221b Baker Street, NW1 6XE
Tel: 020 7224 3688
www.sherlock-holmes.co.uk
* Baker Street

Somerset House
Strand, WC2R 0RN
Tel: 020 7845 4600
www.somersethouse.org.uk
* Temple/Covent Garden

Tate Modern
Bankside, SE1 9TG
Tel: 020 7887 8888
www.tate.org.uk
* Southwark/Blackfriars or
boat 'Tate to Tate' between Tate
Britain, London Eye and Tate
Modern

Tower Bridge
Tower Bridge Road, SE1 2UP
Tel: 020 7403 3761
www.towerbridge.org.uk
* Tower Hill

Tower of London
Tower Hill, EC3N 4AB
Tel: 020 3166 6000
www.hrp.org.uk/tower-of-london
* Tower Hill

Trooping the Colour
From Buckingham Palace, SW1
along the Mall to Horse Guards
Parade, Whitehall and back
again
Time: The Queen's official
birthday (2nd Sat in June) at
11.00am
www.householddivision.org.uk/
trooping-the-colour
*# Charing Cross/ * Westminster

Victoria and Albert Museum
Cromwell Road, South
Kensington, SW7 2RL
Tel: 020 7942 2000
www.vam.ac.uk
* South Kensington

Westminster Abbey
Parliament Square, SW1P 3PA
Tel: 020 7222 5152
www.westminster-abbey.org
* Westminster/ St James's Park

Westminster Cathedral
Francis Street, SW1P 1QW
Tel: 020 7798 9055
www.westminstercathedral.
org.uk
*# Victoria

Windsor Castle
Windsor, Berkshire, SL4 1NJ
Tel: 020 7766 7304
www.royalcollection.org.uk/visit/
windsorcastle
Windsor

**Winston Churchill's Britain at
War Experience**
64–66 Tooley Street, SE1 2TF
Tel: 020 7403 3171
www.britainatwar.co.uk
*# London Bridge

Although every care has been
taken in producing accurate
information for this list, the
publishers cannot accept
responsibility for any errors or
omissions.

*Travel information and ticket
purchasing*
Transport for London Visitor
Centres
Various locations – check
website for details: https://tfl.
gov.uk/fares-and-payments/
where-to-top-up-and-buy-
tickets/visitor-centres

Main Tourist Information Centres
**City of London Information
Centre**
St Paul's Churchyard, EC4M 8BX
Tel: 020 7332 3456
www.visitthecity.co.uk
Open: Mon-Sat: 9:30-5:30
Sun: 10:00-4:00
* St Paul's/Mansion House

**Greenwich Tourist Information
Centre**
Pepys House, 2 Cutty Sark
Gardens, SE10 9LW
Tel: 0870 608 2000
www.greenwich.gov.uk
Open: daily 10.00–17.00

**Royal Windsor Information
Centre**
Windsor Royal Shopping, The
Old Booking Hall, Windsor Royal
Shopping, Thames Ave, Windsor,
SL4 1PJ
Tel: 01753 743900
http://www.windsor.gov.uk/
Open: daily 10.00–16.00
Windsor

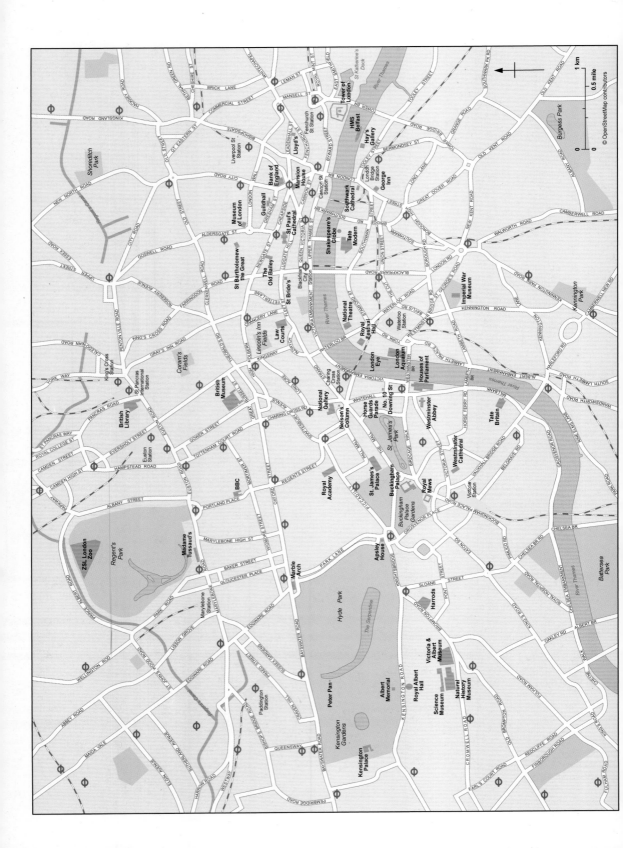